Hi, I'm Kennedy and I'm helping my mom in the garden today!"

"My mom wants my help with dessert tonight, will you please help me get ten apples from the tree?"

"Here is my basket, will you help me shake the tree to see how many apples fall?"

"FOUR, FIVE, SIX!"

"With your help I have collected all ten apples from the tree, thank you!"

"Kennedy the apple pie is ready!"

I Can Count To 20, And So Can You!
Part 2

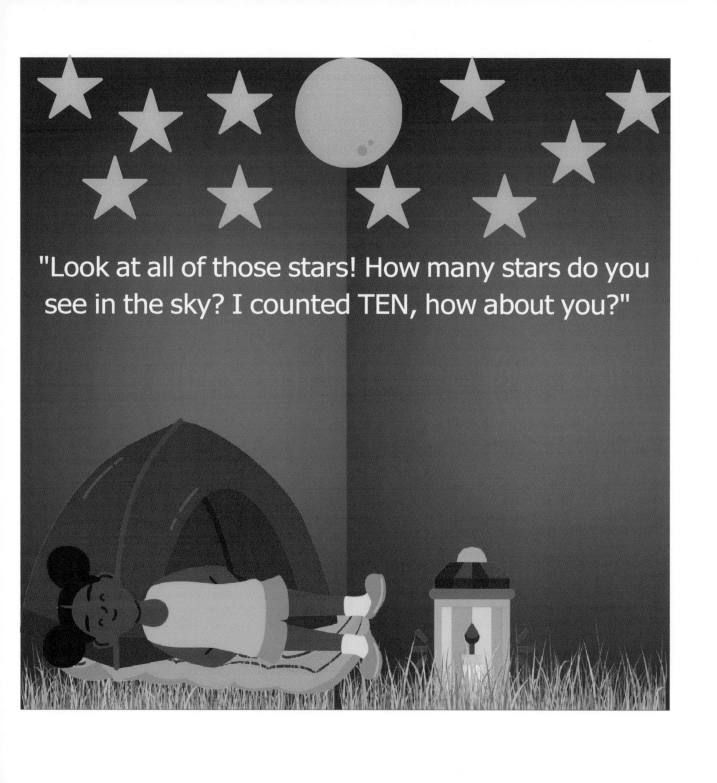

"My mom started a camp fire, can you help me count out 5 marshmallows so we can enjoy s'mores"?

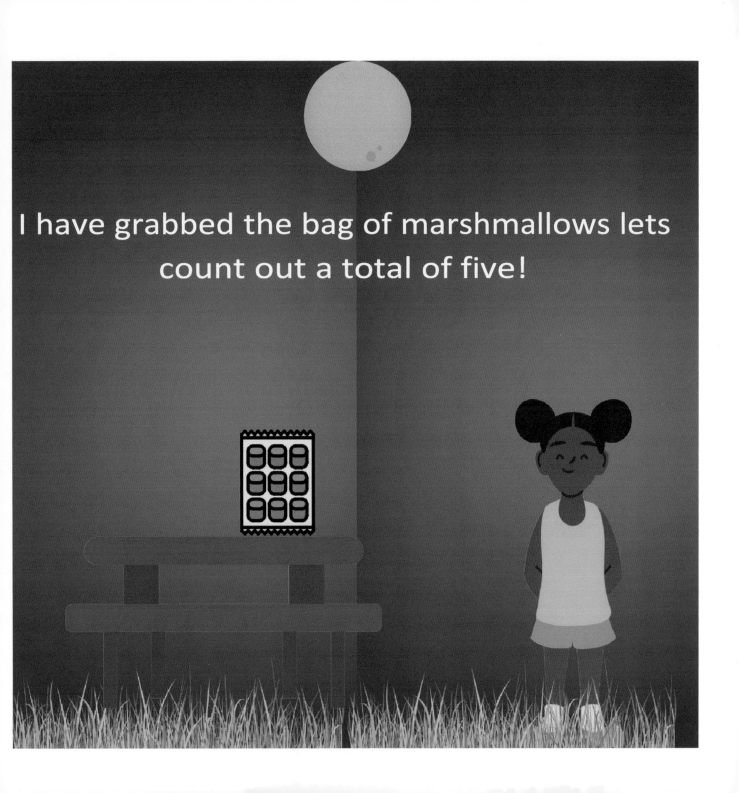

"I have placed five marshmallows on the plate, how many do you see? I see five marshmallows looking at me!"

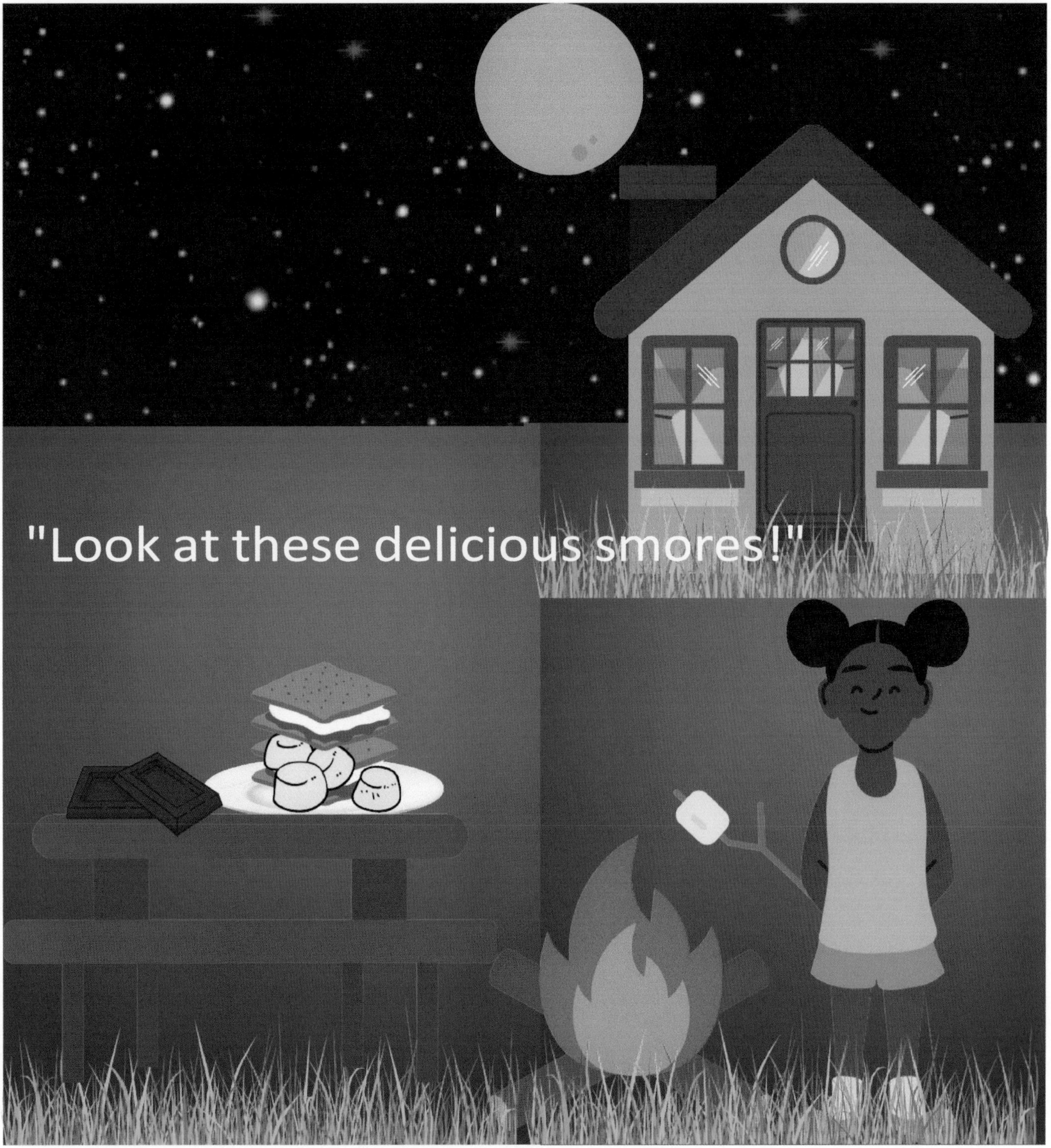
"Look at these delicious smores!"

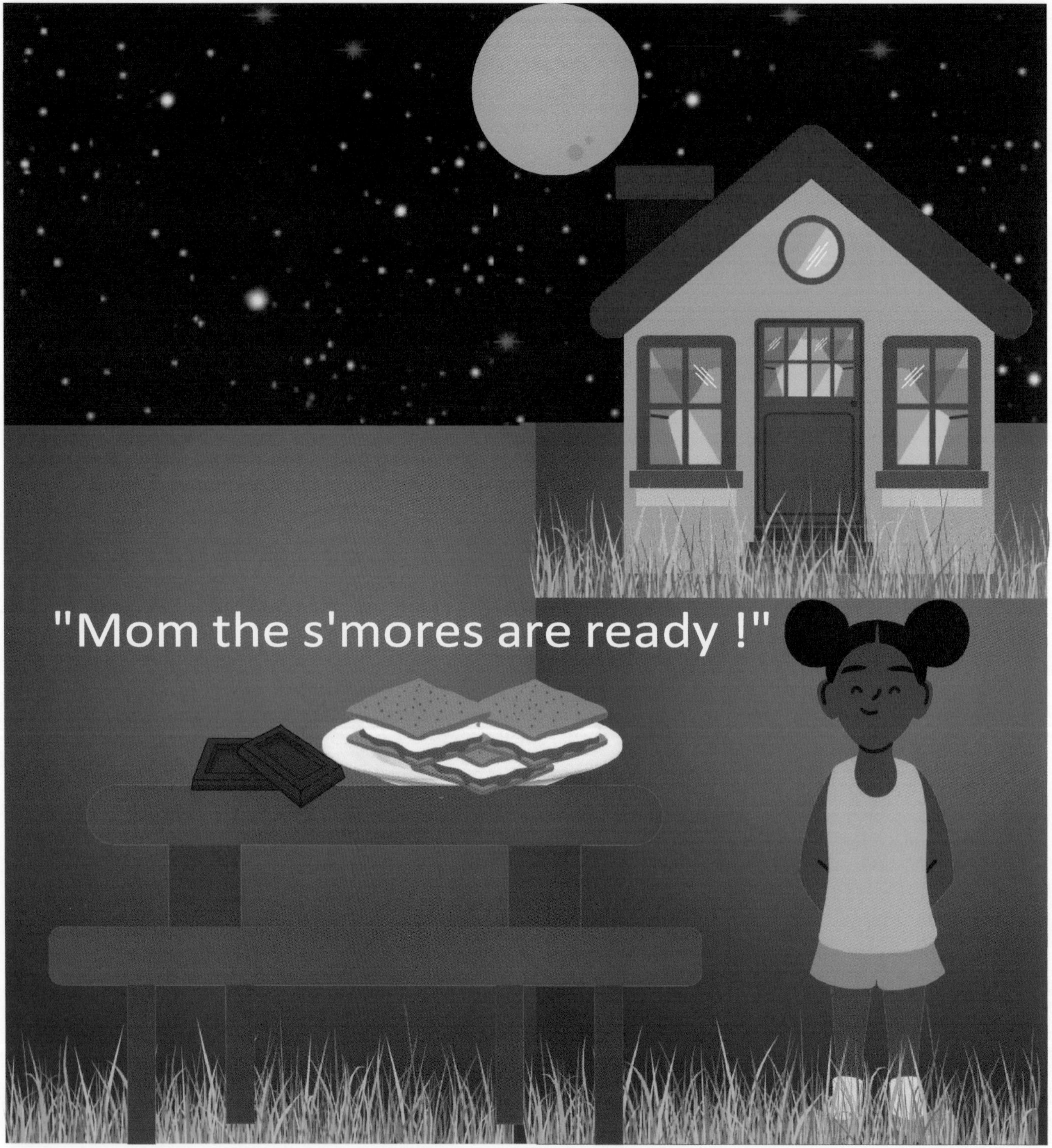
"Mom the s'mores are ready !"

Printed in Great Britain
by Amazon

15528037R00016